I am enough

& other wisdom for
daily living

Also by Margaret Stortz

Flights into Life

Start Living Every Day of Your Life

I am enough

& other wisdom for
daily living

MARGARET STORTZ

Science of **Mind** Publishing
Los Angeles, California

Dedication

To my mother,
whose love for me was constant.

Acknowledgments

To my husband, the most natural man I know, and our blended family, which taught me the exercise of real love and patience. I am grateful also to Science of Mind and its life-affirming, lifesaving philosophy and for every teacher of mine who has walked a part of the way with me.

Made possible by a generous gift from Fran H. Tuchman, in memory of Ralph G. Tuchman, D.D.

Foreword

I LOVE BOTH READING AND WRITING PERSONAL SPIRITUAL essays. So it was with much pleasure that I opened myself to the words in Margaret Stortz's new book *I Am Enough*. I have the habit of letting a book open at will, where it wants to, and direct me to what I need to learn, recollect, reconfirm, or remember. Imagine my delight when I opened to Margaret's essay "On Being Enough." I had recently written an essay on the same subject for *A Soulworker's Companion* and I could only shake my head in wonder at the synchronicity of the universe, where ideas abound until, reaching critical mass, they burst into form on the written page.

Margaret Stortz has this to say about being enough: "In the quiet acceptance of 'enoughness now' lies our inner power to choose to be responsible and responsive to life. We put ourselves in the forefront in that way and stop giving our power away to someone or something else that we may consider more enough than us."

As I browsed through the beautifully written essays I

felt as though I was coming home to a friend. That is their beauty. Whether she is writing about "When Children Die," "The Language of the Heart," "Never Too Much Love," or "Making Changes," a deep humanity infuses each essay. Many of her readers will relate to a blended family, the loss of a child, encroaching old age, the joy of a mature love, the birth of a grandchild, the gold in a seeming disaster, the fall of heroes, the rebirth of flowers in a blooming season, the lesson in a hurt body.

I collect inspiring quotations. So, evidently, does Margaret. She sprinkles them throughout the book as reminders to us of the wisdom and insights that other writers have experienced and now share with us. From Rainer Maria Rilke we learn "Take your practiced powers and stretch them out until they span the chasm between two contradictions...For the god wants to know himself in you." John Bradshaw tells us "Moving beyond myself is actually an inward journey. Moving within is the journey toward spirituality." And J. Allen Boone sums it all up by telling us: "We are members of a vast cosmic orchestra in which each living instrument is essential to the complementary and harmonious playing of the whole."

Margaret Stortz's words are an integral part of that "vast cosmic orchestra" and we, as readers, are a part of it as well, as we respond to her words and are inspired in our own lives by the ideas presented here.

One essay resonates in my mind as an example of what Margaret is asking us, as readers, to see and respond to. In "Will I Ever Be Sure?" she tells the story of visiting a church in Italy as part of a group of American tourists, and encountering an old woman sitting in church saying her rosary. She expands the essay by musing on the faithful being called to Mecca, the Kashmiri weaver pouring his devotion into his work, and the everyday ways in which she too remembers God. She says: "Perhaps I have been looking outward in envy instead of inward in recollection. Perhaps she of the rosary, seeing my sureness, might nod in recognition." The essay ends with a well-known quotation by Ernest Holmes from *The Science of Mind* in which he tells us: "The Spirit can give us only what we can take; it imparts of itself only as we partake of its nature. It can tell us only what we can understand."

As we partake of Margaret Stortz's words, we will

find within the essays and in the accompanying quotations the understanding, wisdom, and comfort that we seek.

BettyClare Moffatt

I am enough

& other wisdom for
daily living

Why Can't I Know God All the Time?

SOMETIMES I ALMOST FEEL ASHAMED THAT I DO NOT CON-
stantly sense the presence of God. After all this time
and practice I certainly should be more adept, more
open, more able to have clear perceptions. Yet there are
days, often many days, when I seem grossly separated
from the source of my love. I must admit, though, that
some days I do not make the effort to turn away from
the colorful distractions of my mind. Indeed, some of
my morbid imaginings fascinate me with the exquisite-
ness of their power to entertain.

Then there are days when I do make a great effort to
become effortless in my relationship with God, and still
I feel enveloped in an invisible thickness of some sort.
Perhaps I should be mollified in knowing that St.
Augustine, too, wished that the hiding God would not
dance away from him.

Nevertheless my heart's desire is to know God all the
time, and the glimpses, warm as mulled wine, keep me
going. These clear incisions in my cloudy days crack

through the mist with a light so compelling that I am bound to keep questing. Is it truly impossible for the finite to know the Infinite? Can I not become so engrossed in the Whole that I can know no otherness? I do not have the answers to my questions, and it does not matter. It matters only that I long to know God all the time...here, in the timeless home of my heart. Whether I be satisfied or not satisfied, still I light my welcome lamp.

For after all the great religions have been preached and expounded, or have been revealed by brilliant scholars, or have been written in books and embellished in fine language with fine covers, man—all men—is confronted with the Great Mystery.

Luther Standing Bear, Lakota Sioux
The Spiritual Athlete

Who Am I?

IS THIS A RIDICULOUS QUESTION? MY BODY TELLS ME WHO I am when it is tired or hungry or in pain. My mind tells me who I am when I am held captive by its anguish or enthralled by its inspiration. I answer to my name. But these are not who I am. They are a few of my perceptions as to who I am, but they are naught but some of my experiences. When I care for my body, its weariness and discomforts are assuaged. When I give my mind ease, it returns to a state of peace; when I die, my name shall die with me.

No, my experiences are not my entirety, though they may seem to be so because of their momentary capacity to consume me. I know there is Something greater in me that wells up into my experiences and yet obliterates them with another series of experiences following after. There is Something in me greater than the sum of anything I might do, be, or have. There is Something in me that is a long hall, down which I must continue to walk.

A mild frustration is felt at not ever seeing my end in sight, at not being able to contemplate my finished product. But sweeping after the frustration and the contemplation is another wave of myself, bolder and more brash, dearer and more compassionate than all that went before. Therefore, I will live in the question. I will make my peace with what I can never fully know. I will continue to ask: Who am I?

Essentially there is one truth underlying our attempts to describe what is indescribable.

Dhyani Ywahoo, Cherokee
The Spiritual Athlete

Standing Alone

SURELY THERE ARE NO CRASHING COASTAL WATERS MORE majestic than those along the Northern California shorelines. I reflected on this majesty as I stood atop a Mendocino County promontory watching the waters do their will below me. Amidst the wonderful sight there stood a small, monolithic boulder with nothing to do but receive the onslaught of the whopping waves. It seemed so alone, so separated from the snuggle of the green hillsides. Obviously it was not bothered by this arrangement since it continued on, year after year, simply doing what came naturally. Would it have complained if it could have? Actually its solitary standing was rewarded by a crown of tidal wildflowers which, while present on the hillsides, were in no way so resplendent as when they garlanded the lonesome rock.

I think we're not so different from that lonely one, for while we love our families and companies and camping trips with friends, we will from time to time stand

7

alone. Not to groups does enlightened thinking or an awareness of greater possibilities come but to the single, quiet mind whose door is open to a quickened musing. We do not even wonder alike but rather reflect in our own time and on our own fronts—some days bold, other days fearful. In the midst of many people, we hold firm to our own unique place.

Does God crown us with garlands for being Her own curious thinkers, willing to stand against the bashings of complacency? I certainly hope so. To think new thoughts can be lonely sometimes.

There can be no thing that does not have within it the signature of God, the Creator of life, the living substance out of which all particular manifestations of life arise; there is no thing that does not have within it as part of its essence, the imprimatur of God, the creator of all, the Bottomer of existence.

Howard Thurman
With Head and Heart

Then and Now

MY GRANDCHILDREN WILL NOT KNOW THE KIND OF LIFE I knew as a child and a young person growing up. They will not while away some of their years in a pseudo-sequestered seasoning process as their adulthood beckons. They cannot; MTV and incessant news programming will see to that. They will not cast sidelong glances at coming times when they will be older and can leisurely consider cultivating a spiritually conscious life. The future now crashes in upon them and upon all of us at frightening speeds, and there is no time for the ignorant to reach gentle, cumulative plateaus of wisdom. We must all grow up together all at once as diverse yet symbiotic life forms.

Thanks to our ruinous use of splendid technologies, we are now at a critical point in our existence as a living species. But what's the expression about an ill wind that blows no good? At the same time as we approach a crisis, we are also witnessing a great groundswell of interest in our spiritual universality shooting forth among people everywhere in a way never before seen in history. We're scratching the surface of our own infinity and discovering our wisdom and compassion and some truly transformational skills. Can crisis be beautiful? Can our forced collective glimpses into the future awaken our awareness that we share a Cosmic Mind? This is the Mind that threads its unitive Self into greatly individualized cultures, which must join together in peace. One day the pearl of great price may finally shine forth.

We can choose to recognize interconnectedness and interrelatedness of all creation and balance our sense of individual, surface-lived separateness with a knowledge of our deeper, spiritual oneness.

William R. Bryant, Jr.
Quantum Politics

Why Me?

EVER WONDERED, WHY ME? EVER LOOK THROUGH WHAT seemed to be a disaster of some proportion and uttered this dismal cry? More than likely we'd be hard pressed to find someone who hasn't wailed in wonder at the vicissitudes of life. A lot less likely, I'll wager, would be one of us speaking forth to say, why not me? None of us ever wishes to feel that difficulties should make their way to our doorstep, let alone be invited in.

Yet, at some level, are we not making this subtle invitation, out of some form of ignorance or despair? Can anyone say in truth that we are not? Not really. We know so little of who we are and how we affect the larger life with which we interact.

Nature is a great teacher if we're willing to consider her simplicity. Do the rocks complain to the tumbling ocean waters that pound them incessantly? Does the eagle sulk because its nests belong in the high, harsh regions of the Earth? And does it wonder why it will surely lose at least one chick to the elements? Well, we can say, these creatures cannot know what lies ahead. Perhaps not, but this lack of knowledge does not keep them from proceeding to be what they are.

With all our supposed abilities to take charge of our thinking, to leap forward in the imagination, why are we not proceeding to be what we are? Could it be that simple steps taken daily, free from the familiar morbidities of thought, might cause the "why me's" to become unnecessary?

The universe is impersonal. It gives alike to all. It is no respecter of persons. It values each alike. Its nature is to impart, ours to receive. When we stand in the light, we cast a shadow across the pathway of our own experience.

Ernest Holmes
The Science of Mind

Love Is a Simple Thing

MANY LOVE SONGS OOZE WITH SMARMY COUPLETS ABOUT the one beloved, but there is one title from a song of yesteryear which can be considered meaningful, for it announces that love is a simple thing. And it is. Really. The longer I live the more I discover that real love, love rooted in the cosmos, is unfussable. In the midst of the toughest circumstances, it can quietly show up almost unnoticed in a look or in the stroke of a hand. No fuss. Just love.

From St. Paul's classic letter to the people of Corinth in which he spoke of love, I have always enjoyed the sentence wherein he suggests that love vaunteth not itself. In other words, it doesn't thrust itself in your face saying, "Look at me, look at me." It silently fills all the spaces of our lives with itself, given the chance.

When my husband gently and meticulously trims and wires his bonsai, there is love in his hands. Every miniature receives the greatest care, the most cautious trims with his tiny clippers. All our children are grown and busy with their own lives, and while my husband loves them passionately, they are no longer needful of his special molding. Here, in these tiny productions, are new children waiting to be formed by his special artistry, his love.

Love is a simple thing. Through it God creates with a silent touch. There are no announcements, no fanfares, just the occasional melody of the universal Song humming in our ears of its love.

Effortlessly
Love flows from God into man
Like a bird
Who rivers the air
Without moving her wings.
Thus we move in His world,
One in body and soul,
Though outwardly separate in form.
As the Source strikes the note,
Humanity sings.

Mechtild of Magdeburg
The Enlightened Heart

Speaking of Failure

GOD, HOW I HATE TO FAIL! AT ANYTHING! IT SEEMS I HAVE to make all sorts of explanations to myself about why things did not turn out the way I had planned; and if I've made a public spectacle of myself, I have to smile while well-meaning folks make their way to me carrying invisible stretchers to buoy me up. Besides all this I feel foolish and vulnerable, and then guilt keeps me awake nights. What did I do wrong? I should have known better...and the mother of all guilts: maybe God didn't want me to succeed.

How we do love to torment ourselves, as if God is sitting around deciding who does or does not get the goodies. That's a pretty capricious God, I'd say...a lot like my Uncle Ray. It's a heck of a thing to have to admit, but failure is probably at least as good a teacher as success—possibly even better, at least from our current perspectives. Failure stirs things up. It gets us to thinking more sharply (once we stop complaining, of course), and maybe even leads to an awareness of the tremendous gap between what we thought we knew about ourselves and what we really know. Gaps have a tendency to get filled in with something we had never thought about before, even a gem or two.

It is said that God is always bringing us gifts. Could it be that some of them come in the form of an occasional failure?

Break down everything except the recognition of the one perfect Power, which is not contingent upon any place, person, condition, time of year, or anything but itself.

Ernest Holmes
The Science of Mind

He, She, and It

THESE ARE INTERESTING TIMES TO BE TALKING ABOUT GOD, for we now find ourselves groping for terms that suggest greater universality and equality. One might say we are seeking the most "spiritually correct" way to refer to God. To call God "He" can be regarded as chauvinistic and smacks of the old paternalistic impositions made upon believers. We could refer to God as "She" to please certain people, but we might also get some snickering from those who take their spirituality very seriously and who might consider this term equally unrepresentative of an all-inclusive Deity. Then there is the grand "It," which term might not offend anyone but might not garner much inspiration either.

We can make things easy for ourselves by remembering that God really just *is*. Which pronoun we use is of no concern to God. Each preference is right, the masculine as well as the feminine, and the rationalist also has a good point to make in this whole derring-do.

Whatever sweet pronoun appeals to us is the one to be used, since it is the strong, personal sense of tuning in to our Unity with God that we want most ardently anyway; and here we are not even considering other endearing intimacies used by some of the more liberal-minded people, such as Old Dear or Big Sweetie! Wouldn't these add a few twinkles to the eye!

Besides, God is busy being God, so does He, She, or It care how called or by whom? Or is He creatively responding to Her manifest creation while merrily doing Its thing?

Self is everywhere, shining forth from all beings,
vaster than the vast, subtler than the most subtle,
unreachable, yet nearer than breath, than heartbeat.

The Upanishads
The Enlightened Heart

Incidental or Integral

MOST OF US HAVE DAYS WHEN WE DON'T FEEL WORTH A hoot! Things are not going our way and we get discouraged. I know. I've had a few of these days. At such times it is hard to feel that we are an integral part of the creative process. Yet we are. The premises of quantum physics, among other disciplines, tell us of the interconnectedness of all that exists in the universe. Everything does interact with and affect everything else, no matter how subtly. Not a sparrow falleth but God does not know. It seems staggering to realize that this is more than a quaint piece of imagery.

The story is told of a man who, having suffered greatly during WWI, hid himself in a barren section of land in France. A century or so before, the area had been completely deforested and had never been restored. As the man began to heal, he determined to do some good in his life, so he elected to plant one hundred acorns every day in that stricken land. This was no small task since he had to walk many miles to gather the acorns. In time, the oaks began to grow, not all of course, but the man continued to plant. Before long, the birds and insects that accompanied such forestation began to appear. Even streams started to form until eventually a whole ecosystem was restored, all due to the efforts of one man who wanted to make a difference.

This story is appealing, but not unique. We are reminded of other singular individuals who, through intention, create remarkable beauty. Not any one of us is less than these.

A billion stars go spinning through the night,
blazing high above your head.
But in you is the presence that
will be, when all the stars are dead.

Rainer Maria Rilke
The Enlightened Heart

Creativity

My spirit, like water,
Takes the forms my mind describes.
Sometimes beautiful,
Sometimes not.
Sometimes, in its hardness,
My heart designs brittle days
Which cannot turn corners.

When not frozen,
My heart marries upward
And joins my mind in glory.
Visions are lustrous,
Taking form and breath.
And I am closer to the softness
Of my Spirit.

The shutters are opened
To views not before seen.
My chisel is not needed.
Just the lightest words
Perform the miracle now.

On Being Enough

ONE OF OUR CURRENT POPULAR APHORISMS IS SO STATED: I am enough. This sounds all well and good, but in what way do we seem to be enough? Is it in the possession of physical loveliness? I have known people who were generally considered breathtakingly beautiful yet who did not consider themselves to be enough—and no one could convince them otherwise. I have also watched very ordinary-looking people captivate audiences of thousands. Physical beauty is an asset certainly, but enoughness does not lie there.

Does great intelligence provide enoughness? One might think so, but we have all known those gifted with brilliance who did not fulfill themselves. We can look in many areas for proofs of our enoughness, something we can weigh or measure that tells the world we are enough.

There is much confusion between just being enough and achieving something that proves our worth, between being enough inwardly and appearing good

23

on the outside. Perhaps enoughness is much simpler than that. Perhaps we need only awaken each morning and take a breath without looking for that great, external thing which announces us to the world as being enough.

In the quiet acceptance of "enoughness now" lies our inner power to choose to be responsible and responsive to life. We put ourselves in the forefront that way and stop giving our power away to someone or something else that we may consider more enough than us.

In our enoughness lies the ability to live with the insecurity of being unable to be certain we are enough! This is a paradoxical notion but for now, it is enough!

Science can never provide any complete and definitive understanding of reality—theology can never provide a complete and definite understanding of divine mysteries.

Fritjof Capra and David Steindl-Rast
Belonging to the Universe

Remembrances of War

IT HAS BEEN AN ABILITY OF MINE TO EXPERIENCE AND TO observe at the same time, and while recently visiting the USS *Arizona* Memorial in Pearl Harbor, I was able to do both in abundance. During the introductory film Lowell Thomas's narrations on *Movietone News* rewound me right back into my wartime childhood. There in black and white, on someone's home movies, we viewers all raced back over fifty years to watch a floating fortress explode into a steel mausoleum in a matter of minutes. I found that I was not so inured by modern-day violence as to be impervious to the magnitude of the massive dying. I stifled a sob.

During the launch ride over to the memorial itself the hundred or so of us were all very quiet, unduly courteous to one another. Even the very young, for whom this visit could have little meaning, shuffled noiselessly in their seats. We disembarked onto the airy, sloping white building as *Arizona's* shadowy skeleton rested below us, rusting gun turrets standing like sentinels above the surface of the water.

It was almost anomalous to see this sun-filled white bridge astride its sunken galleon, so much life guarding so much death. Then we entered the Shrine Room, and clearly, in stark lettering, stood forth 1,177 names of men who were alive one minute and dead the next, including *Arizona's* captain and a divisional rear admiral. Like those of a much newer memorial in Washington, D.C., its walls were continually draped with flowers in adoration and regret.

The only consistent sound inside the memorial was the slap, slap, slap of a rope against a flagpole whose colors were at half-mast that day (a former president had just died). There were questions for the park rangers and musings among us, but the quiet tone endured, encouraged perhaps by the stalking shadows of death below us.

On the way back to the harbor's shores I was struck by the easy, ongoing flow of the green waters of the Pacific. It held all the tears of those who had mourned not only *Arizona's* dead but those who had been killed before and since; and with seeming effortlessness it stood ready to hold the tears yet to come.

I wondered…is there something to know that we do not now know? We know that all the oceans of the world tirelessly gather our tears without disrupting their tide tables one jot. We know that the earth patiently receives the bodies of those who die too soon and yet never fails to follow its seasonal course. The cosmic Architect lures the sun and moon into their orbits just as it has done through untold millennia. It is we who must awaken now to the unceasing call of life within us to let itself be lived in marvelous ways. Creativity is its medium, not murder. We have misunderstood this altogether, and we have our lonely memorials to remind us of our terrible excesses.

Tomorrow will dawn as it always has, and the paths of our destinies will beckon as they have always done. They are ours to walk now as thinkers, lovers, and creators, the methods of war banished from our memories forever. I saw these possibilities in the eyes of a young Japanese visitor on *Arizona's* bridge as she took my hand in friendship. I lodge them in my being as the only alternatives my heart will accept.

And they shall beat their swords into plowshares, and their spears into pruning hooks...neither shall they learn war any more.

Isaiah 2:4

Why Am I Afraid to Love?

WHY AM I AFRAID TO BE LOVING AT TIMES? AM I AFRAID I'LL lose something of myself or that I'll become too vulnerable? I think about these questions and then try to remember what I know. Now, I know that I should secure my dotted-line personal boundaries, even though I live a larger, infinite life. I know that I still want to carve out my private piece, my pocket garden self, and tend to it. It's good that I do these things. I am, after all, the only one who can think my thoughts, feel my feelings, and make my choices.

Honestly, I fully believe that I have a taproot into endless Love and that I'll never, ever run out; yet I sometimes act as if I have only so much love to give and that if I tried to love according to my endless inheritance, I might wear out. Such logic is strangely contradictory. I speak of my endlessness and of my wearing out in the same breath.

Of course I want to be loved in return, and this desire, too, contradicts the unceasingness of my love. If my loving is rooted in infinite givingness, why should I care who returns it and who doesn't? That wouldn't stop my loving, if I lived what I know of myself.

Here's the crux, perhaps. Maybe I *don't* know what I *think* I know. Or maybe I know a part of what I think I know but not all of what I think I know. Very curious...and it's back to the drawing board, but then love is a very sweet board to draw on.

Love asks no questions. Its natural state is one of extension and expansion, not comparison and measurement.

Gerald Jampolsky
Love is Letting Go of Fear

30

Nonresistance

I ONCE KNEW A MAN WHO WAS SO WISE THAT HE NEVER fought with his ex-wife! Never! I recall being on hand at times when they would talk by telephone while she read him the riot act left and right. In fact I remember on one of these occasions actually hearing her voice come through the receiver and into the space around him so that others could catch her words. That was loud talking!

Yet he never raised his voice, never interrupted the rising flow of words until the woman had emptied herself of all she had to say at that time and finally hung up the telephone. To my astonished look he replied, "If you close the door to the buffeting wind, it will beat against the door. If you open all the doors and windows, the wind, meeting no resistance, will spend itself." Here was a man who knew the magic of nonresistance.

More than that, the man also spoke to the woman with great consideration and genuine understanding

31

for her feelings and seemed to shed the harsh commentary with small effort. Eventually the two of them became able to speak to each other with true cordiality, if not affection. Could this be what the Master meant when he said, "Resist not evil, but return good for evil instead"?

At some level my friend certainly knew something about the Universal Law as he set a new relationship in motion with patience and kindness rather than continuing to perpetuate a difficult one by returning anger for anger.

Possibly we could all learn something from him.

With all the variables involved it is little wonder that communication is difficult. It takes all the effort of both speaker and listener to make it work. It takes mindfulness.

William Bryant, Jr.
Quantum Politics

When Children Die

WHEN CHILDREN DIE, OUR NOTIONS OF THE APPROPRIATENESS of death always seem to go out the window. It seems so unnatural that the young should ever die! One is supposed to grow up, reach adulthood, experience the lessons of life—and then die, full of years, the body used up. What a grating experience it is to look upon the face of a young person lying in repose and know that those shining eyes will never again open.

I remember standing at the bedside of a young girl who had just died as the result of a serious accident. She was without blemish except for the fact that her head was swathed in a turban of bandages. She still had the rosiness of her youth in her cheeks. One expected her to awaken at any moment from some sweet reverie, ready to share it all with us.

It is these times which clap us alongside the head to remind us of the tenuousness of our physical self. There is, after all, a part of us which cannot stay forever, and young death drives us all into great internal searching to find what we truly believe. Is life durable? Can we so easily be deprived of it, and will I see my beautiful child again?

None but our own soul can satisfy our longings, our desires to be healed, to be happy again, to be assured that nothing, no matter how upsetting, will disturb our link with cosmic Love. That we can ever smile again has always been evidence to me that Love does regenerate our will and heal our heart. When a soft hand wipes away a tear, surely God's extension is in that kind gesture.

Am I the thoughts that float in brain stuff
held within bone walls?
Or the two-legged creature who carries
that brain stuff and bone bindings?
Or a collection of experiences
that give rise to those thoughts?
Or the beings that cause
those experiences to happen?
Or the earth that caused
those beings to exist?

Or the cosmos from which earth sprang?
Or the light from which
the cosmos blossomed?
If I am any one of these
then I am also every one of these,
And I shall have everlasting life.

The Green Bible

Tell Me

Tell me.
Tell me what I already know.
Speak to me of the cosmic Self in me.
Remind me again that God is more than my aware-
ness,
That the forces of Mind never desert my thoughts.

Sing again the phrases which call forth my belief
And make me stand fast in silent devotion
When I have forgotten everything.

Don't scowl or press hard.
Don't cast your eyes askance.
Be the vessel of my knowing
For just a brief while
As I gather up the pieces of my mind
So scattered from my tumble.

Smile.
Love me,
And tell me softly what I already know.

Strange and Wonderful

I ADMIT THAT I HAVE NOT ALWAYS BEEN OPEN TO THAT which I considered strange. Things had to fit together and be workable. Everything had to serve some obvious purpose. In the world of what I viewed to be proper religious practices I could not see the reason some people had for not engaging in any physical activity on their Sabbath. I could not imagine the efficacy of shaking a prayer wheel or positioning a prayer rug in just a certain way. There seemed no commonsense purpose to these rituals.

However, over time I have awakened to the world beyond common sense and discovered a whole layer of unconscious, mythic patterns that cast a long, long shadow upon the way we do just about everything. Apparently we are not just who we think we are. We are made up of the religious-cultural-social overtones of all that has gone before us, and these influences affect not only our approach to life but even the way we carry our bodies.

Underneath all is the ground of the only One, we believe, but the road to this wholeness is marked by footsteps wearing strange and wonderful sandals, and along the way, a swaying dance of devotion to the One danced in bare feet.

Humans, separated by mutual fear and distrust, unite by forging bonds based on openness, friendship, trust, genuine respect, and love. Previously separated parts of the system are brought together, creating unanticipated levels of success and hybrid vitality.

George Land and Beth Jarman
Breakpoint and Beyond

The Language of the Heart

The language of the heart,
While saying nothing,
Transmits everything.

AS I WATCH MY HUSBAND WORDLESSLY PERFORMING A small chore, I feel that, should I simply look toward him, he would know exactly what I am thinking. I follow the softness of his movements out of the corner of my eye and, while I am not directly observing him, I know what he is doing. For my part, I am engaging in a small bit of necessary reading and have no current need for or interest in conversation. For several minutes the room is silent, comfortable, warmed by our two presences, and entirely inviting. One could fall asleep and feel completely secure.

My husband interrupts the silence to say, "You know, it's enough just to be here with you. I could work on anything this way." The One Mind strikes again!

Scientists are busily formulating a grand theory of

unification, trying to prove that all cosmic activity comes from one source. Nice of them to spend their time this way, and it will certainly help to describe that which has been ineffable up until now; but I already know about this Unity. Anyone who has ever loved and been loved does. How else does one account for the inspiration of an entire story in a single look?

There is a kind of underground communication going on among people all the time, and sometimes verbal language obstructs more than it clarifies. When we grow to know and trust each other it becomes a simple matter to come together at the silent, deep levels of our communal livingness...the language of the heart.

We are members of a vast cosmic orchestra in which each living instrument is essential to the complementary and harmonious playing of the whole.

J. Allen Boone
Kinship with All Life

Deep Waters

MY MIND FASCINATES ME! I AM AMAZED AT ALL THE NOTIONS I can conjure up when left to my own devices. I can call up slights, real or imagined, that happened to me years ago and enlarge upon them enormously if I really feel like creating a "pity fit" for myself. Where does all this old stuff come from?

The mind is a wondrous thing. A property of cosmic Being, it is individualized in its many living forms, some of which are we humans—which is when the fun begins. We do get to dream and to despair as we will, and whatever we have thought and felt enters into what I call the deep waters of the mind. Although all metaphors for the mind fall short, I liken our human mind to a great body of water. We see fairly clearly what lies at the surface; but as our thoughts lengthen into memory, they drop deeply into the darker, more obscure levels, perhaps not to resurface until some internal upheaval makes them bubble upward.

The denizens of our deeps are varied and curious.

Some thoughts, like blind fish, cannot stand the light at the surface. They must be replaced. Others glow with their own light and lend an inherent vitality wherever they go. They illumine the mind, and we love them for it. Then there are the rotting hulks, old, set patterns which we may have to dredge out of the mud through our spiritual practices, our own private "cranes."

Maybe we should scuba dive more often!

We are going into deep outer space based on developments of modern technology. However, there are many things left to be examined and thought about with respect to the nature of the mind, what the substantial core of the mind, what the corroborative condition of the mind is...

The Dalai Lama
Oceans of Wisdom

Ode to a Hummingbird

U, Hummingbird, why do you fly?
'Fraid the food cart won't come by?
With flowers and feeders ever nigh,
Seems that you're unsure as I.

IN RECENT YEARS WE HAVE BEEN DELIGHTED WITH THE antics of our local hummingbirds, since we now have two feeders in our front yard. It's quite interesting to see how pugnacious and territorial they can become, even to the point of dive-bombing one another if some unwelcome visitor gets too close to the feeders. In fact one little fellow likes to lie in wait inside the folds of a nearby leafy bush, ready to run off any who would drink from "his" feeder.

They cannot know that there will be plenty of food for them all. They cannot know that the Birdfeeder God, my husband, loves to make certain the feeders are always full; so they fight over what they perceive is a limited amount which must be theirs alone.

Come to think of it, we humans can sometimes be a lot like the hummers. We either do not know or keep forgetting that we live in the bounteous lap of a universal Presence whose joy it is to fulfill its creation; and in our dull-mindedness, we fight for every piece of good, thinking there'll never be enough to go around.

The hummer cannot take thought about that which is greater than himself, but we can. Five billion human beings cannot lie in wait for one another without creating disastrous results, but they can conceive of a good life for all. They can know of the Power, greater than they are, which is endlessly available to all, and learn to use it with love, wisdom, and for the benefit of all.

The Call and the Way

THERE IS BUT ONE CALL. THERE ARE MANY WAYS TO THE call. The call to be is indigenous to everything that lives. Birds, fish, and animals, less complicated than humans, are always heeding the call to be what they are as they wing through the air, swirl through the waters of Earth, or pad the trails of the globe. They do not engage in polemics over which way is right, and we do not question their ways. We're wise enough not to want fish to fly like birds.

We will not give this same consideration to ourselves, however. We tend to want to homogenize our traditions, our cultures, and our religions. There is, of course, a right way to do things! Or so we say.

What we may not be recognizing is that the way must match the call. The call cannot be asked to match the way. My call to be is, for instance, not as Catholic. Yet I thrill to the power of piety in the Mass celebrated by those people who are called to march to that drum. I would feel it rude to impose the informalities of my call upon those deeply attuned to the rituals of their own calls.

Many roads lead to Rome, and magnificent they all are. Dr. Matthew Fox, the great theologian, once suggested that we live in post-denominational times and quipped that there are no Catholic oceans or Baptist rain forests. Possibly we could tread one another's way from time to time to discover the great Earth that calls to each.

It is idolatrous to over identify the Spirit of the divine One with any one form or expression of forms.

Matthew Fox
The Coming of the Cosmic Christ

Will I Ever Be Sure?

WHILE VISITING IN ITALY, I AND A GROUP OF AMERICAN tourists happened upon an old, bandanna'd woman sitting in church saying her rosary. I could see her lips move soundlessly through her mysteries as she fingered each worn bead in a well-remembered ritual. Our clattering did not disrupt her one jot, so intent were her devotions. Later on, I wondered if I would ever know my God as well as she knew hers. I imagined that, through her long life, her ancient rosary guided her through the good times and the bad. Did my faith have that same certainty?

I have seen videos of the faithful being called to prayer by the intonations of the muezzin reminding all of the greatness of God. Without hesitation, every face turned toward Mecca; every forehead touched the ground in abject surrender. Will I ever be that sure? If I were a Kashmiri weaving his complex designs, could I weave my heart of devotion in the threads of the unfolding rug?

47

Some days I am sure, when the breath of God breezes past my cheek as I walk and when I place my energy-dispensing hand upon someone's pained limb to feel him relax into comfort. When my beloved and I dissolve a quarrel instantly with one quiet touch, I am sure. When I sit in my temple and melt into the surroundings, I am sure. Perhaps these are my prayer rugs, my rosary. Perhaps I have been looking outward in envy instead of inward in recollection. Perhaps she of the rosary, seeing my sureness, might nod in recognition.

The Spirit can give us only what we can take; it imparts of itself only as we partake of its nature. It can tell us only what we can understand.

Ernest Holmes
The Science of Mind

48

It's Spring

WHAT IS THERE ABOUT THE FIRST SMELL OF SPRING THAT makes me feel so young? No matter how I may have been feeling in previous days, when those warm, bright days shed a little sun on my winter-withered body, I fill out again with smiles and expectations that could keep a five-year-old running to catch up! It's almost as if some cosmic imp has breathed in my ear, "Time to wake up, old dear!"

I think there must be an irresistible allure attached to those tiny buds pushing through the sleeping bark of the trees in our front yard. There is almost a compulsion in me to take a daily peek at the fragile, jewel-like tips shooting forth from our yawning filigree maples. Maybe this is what is meant by the great axiom, "Deep calls to deep." I expect so. I believe that somehow all Life is continually calling to itself, though we don't always listen.

But let's give ourselves a little more credit now. We do know that the renewal of spring is as great a soul event as it is a season in nature. We are nature's children, and the changing seasons replay themselves in us consistently. The best part of this internal eventfulness is that we can declare which season we shall experience. Do we want quiet reflection? Come, winter! Perhaps in an hour our passions will be engaged full bore in the heat of creativity. March in, summer! Or, if we are in the mood to make a flower necklace, enter spring!

That the sun shines
And the planets turn,
That a seed sprouts
And the flowers blossom,
That the water flows downhill
And the winds blow,
These things are God
And they are also God's laws.

Carl Christensen
The Green Bible

High Flying

I REMEMBER WITH GREAT PLEASURE A HABIT ONE OF MY SONS had as a small boy. At that time we owned a large, broad-backed chair, upon which he would regularly climb to sit backward and gaze out the window. There was a great expanse of yard within the range of his vision, almost like a meadow, and unobstructed sky. Yet I knew that he was seeing something more vast than anything that lay before him. His eyes were bright, but his inner vision was turned in. I loved to watch him, and I always tried not to disturb him while his mind took him wherever it would.

In later years I ran across a term used by Joseph Chilton Pierce called a "gate-ing mechanism," which he explained as the ability of children to shift out of their mundane environments into another boundless world of being. This, he believed, they could do willfully, easily, and with great flexibility. I came to feel that this was what my little one was doing, although my term for it was "high flying."

I never knew where he went in his flights or what he found there. He never spoke of them to me, and perhaps it was appropriate that he did not. It was, after all, his secret place of the Most High and not mine. It also occurred to me that perhaps he could not. Perhaps there were no words to capture the essence of his fancies.

It interests me that some of our memories slip away from us readily—and some never lose their luster. This one, for me, never dims—and never will.

We are constantly invited to be what we are.

Henry David Thoreau

Moments in Meditation

SCATTERED...TOGETHER...SCATTERED...TOGETHER. THESE are oftentimes the kinds of movements my mind makes as I engage in my contemplations. Now I sink deeply into the utter stillness of belonging, nothing and no one presenting themselves for attention. Now the wild horses of my thoughts flee from serenity as though racing before a prairie fire.

Scattered...together...scattered...together. Now moving cleanly and ever so easily from one thought to another as if vaulting through time in slow motion, now wondering why this person, who presumably is in control of her thoughts, does not control her thoughts. So it is when one meditates, it seems, but I have come to live with the outrageous wanderings for the times when I knife through to the quiet spot that waits for me.

Through it all I have come to know that God is present as much in the insecurities of my mind as in the stance of quietude which appears more Godlike. I find this knowledge comforting and a very great incentive to keep on corralling the wild horses. Once I used to berate myself for the inability to hone in on the quiet place within myself more quickly and easily. I supposed I should be doing better since I had spent so many years in spiritual studies. Then in a moment of stillness encapsulated within one of my more turbulent sittings, the thought pierced through the rumbling that God is all the same whether I am in a place of sufficiency or not. My regrets didn't change one thing. The message of being is always waiting.

We live in a sea of Perfect Life and we should take time to understand and sense this in our imagination.

Ernest Holmes
The Science of Mind

The Language without Words

I HOPE I AM NOT ALONE IN THIS DISCOVERY. ACTUALLY I very much doubt I am because I feel sure many of us have encountered times when the spoken word simply cannot say what we mean to convey. I don't suppose any great analysis is necessary to understand why this is so, for words can be slippery, sliding things, easily manipulated and misrepresentative. Words can be used intentionally to conceal the truth. I believe this is called lying.

Then, too, there are the words that roar forth from us when we are angry, gush forth when we are effusive, barely squeak forth when we are afraid, and are wrung from us in anguished cries when we are sorrowful, all of which may give some indication of what we mean to impart but often just create confusion or misunderstanding. There must be other ways to transmit our meanings more simply, and there are.

God created us with so much depth and with so many sensitivities that it is no wonder we sometimes mix ourselves up. But there is one clear way to convey a message and that is through our touch. When more words seem likely to start a donnybrook, the soft touch of a hand on a person's cheek can cut through anger and communicate a simple "I love you. Don't be misled by my words." Perhaps when the urge to speak comes, we can lightly lift a finger to our lips as if to say, "Hush. No words right now. Let God speak through our touch."

What goes for the world "out there" also goes for the world "in here." They are the same world.

Noel McInnis
You Are an Environment

Come, Whisper in My Ear

Leaping up the stairs,
Hearing the latch snap open,
I'm sure of my heart's love
When my dearest enters the room.

Moving inward,
Probing the depths of my energetic mind.
I'm not sure what my search will bring,
A touch so clear that I cannot mistake my God?
Perhaps so. Perhaps not.

Why is the one so obvious,
The other so elusive?
Must I see tender eyes to feel loved?
Must I be struck to know Oneness?

A shared lament, I'm sure,
The wanting all my way,
Clean, clear, no doubts, no nonsense.
Come, God, whisper in my ear!

Tell me what I long to hear,
That You love me and he loves me.

How foolish.

You are he.

A Perfect Experience

WE ALL HAVE NOTIONS ABOUT HOW SOMETHING PERFECT should look. The trouble is that our ideas about perfection don't quite match. We can define it as that which is without blemish or that to which nothing can be added or taken away from. While these definitions may all be true, they don't help much. One man's blemish is another woman's beauty mark, and we could dance endlessly around the metaphysical concept of completeness.

I seldom call forth my own insistence on perfection because I would probably stop before I began anything. I have come to live nicely with "very good" and an occasional "excellent" since these standards allow me room for accomplishment. But now and again, if rarely, I find myself folded into something that is truly perfect—not because I caused it to be so or judged it to be so but because every particular fell into exactly the right place at the right time of its own accord.

As I began to feel the meaning of perfection rather

than just to think about it, I realized that it is an experience more than a thing and that it is always greater than the sum of its parts. I remember a "perfect" funeral service where a number of disparate situations simply fell together into something that swept up hundreds of people into a pervasive sense of well-being. Considering the skillful effort needed to manage a large public funeral, I am aware that this one could have been either shambles or splendor. Blessedly it was the latter, thanks to its place in a perfect universe.

The truth will out; the Spirit will make itself known. Happy are we if we see these things which, from the foundation of the human race, have been longed for by all aspiring souls.

Ernest Holmes
The Science of Mind

Never Too Much Love

SEVERAL YEARS AGO I DIVORCED THE FATHER OF MY CHIL-
dren after a marriage of many years. Later on I mar-
ried another man, a man who also has children. When
I spoke to my grown children about the impending
marriage, I told them that I was not replacing their
father in any way but that I was bringing one more
person into their lives to love them. However this
intention may have been viewed by our several off-
spring, over time it is exactly what has taken place. All
our children have at least one extra parent loving
them. In my mind no parent, natural or otherwise, was
being diminished, and the life of each one of our children was being enhanced by a greater pool of love
than any of us could have provided alone.

This result was not easy to achieve; it was definitely
no picnic! Both my husband and I had to exercise
much patience and deal with a lot of frustration. We
also had to not mind the fact that some of these
enlarged family frameworks took several years to

accomplish; and though it may sound like the invocation of a grand platitude, love did conquer all. I cannot say that every segment of these multifaceted relationships are perfect or sometimes even entirely comfortable, but they're all alive and well.

It's my belief that no one, especially children, can have enough people loving them, and that it is a waste of possible life-enhancing relationships to burn bridges unnecessarily. Duke Ellington once was quoted as saying that his feet hardly touched the ground until he was about seven years old, so much did relatives lovingly carry him about. I say amen to that!

It seems more accurate to say that one grows in love. The more he learns, the more his opportunities to change his behavioral responses and thus expand his ability to love. Man is either constantly growing in love, or dying.

Leo Buscaglia
Love

Flying Away

I'D LIKE TO FLY AWAY SOMETIMES. AT LEAST I THINK I would. Every now and again a powerful urge strikes me to jump in the car, drive off, and never come back. Then the practical me steps in. What happens when I run out of gas? Or get hungry or lonely? And what about the people who love me? How could I do such a thing to them?

I do have precedence for practicing reasonable restraint, for I have known of people who actually indulged in my musing. They really did fly away or, at least in one case, simply drove off and never came back. I have also seen the broken lives they left behind as they slipped out of their perceived shackles—nice people wondering what in the world was so awful about them that Father had to run off.

As my desire to be comfortable and responsible begins to settle my rebellious mind, I realize that I do not really want to rush off into Never-Never Land...but isn't there a vacation spot somewhere in between, somewhere I could fly for just a little while but run on back when the dinner bell rings? Maybe this little longing in me is one reason why we invented fantasies—so that we could play in our minds but be serious at home. Maybe this is where visions begin—in this little, fertile land.

Thank God for the nonresisting God who lets us fly a little or fly a lot, who seems not to be concerned with any of it and who holds constant welcome to all the flyers.

> *The Tao gives forth to all beings,*
> *nourishes them, maintains them,*
> *cares for them, comforts them, protects them,*
> *takes them back to himself...*

> Lao-tzu
> *The Enlightened Heart*

Useful Pain

PAIN! WHO NEEDS IT? NO ONE, OF COURSE. BUT PAIN IS A part of life from time to time. Sometimes the pain is physical, at other times, mental. Philosopher Ernest Holmes suggests that pain and suffering do not have to be present in our lives and that we can grow from a more enlightened choice than one made out of pain. To me this concept makes perfect sense. We should be able to move from glory to glory. We have the infinite Mind for it! At the same time there is a quiet place in me which whispers, "Nice work if you can get it!"

It's not that I am of two minds about this. It's simply that I don't always seem to remember the glory that is available to me. Therefore I experience pain. One benefit, I suppose, is that it makes me more fully aware of my aliveness, and also serves as an incentive for me to move back to my glory again for healing. And in between? Some of the most beautiful and insightful of all my writings come forth from painful experience, and this interests me. Why should I, a spiritual being, need such a constricted womb from which to birth beautiful things? It seems too mysterious.

I guess I need only look at my beautiful children to answer that question, though. They were certainly worth the pain. Nevertheless, like Holmes, I would rather grow from an enlightened ease, and so I'm working on it. I'll use pain as a tool for learning only if I must.

Face your pain and you are free to do something about it. Deny your pain and you are powerless to do anything that might stop the hurting.

Dr. Bill De Foore
Anger

Angry People

SO MANY PEOPLE SEEM TO BE SORE ABOUT SOMETHING THESE days, and thanks to current therapies a lot of new buzzwords populate our vocabularies now—words like "codependent" and "abusive" and "victim" and "survivor." Maybe these terms are apt descriptions of many circumstances people have endured, and maybe examining their experiences assists people in reclaiming their lives, but a lot of anger and hostility seem to accompany these explorations. As a minister I often feel I must walk on little cat feet in order not to say something which will upset the imminently upsettable, and sometimes I just cannot discern the difference between a needed cathartic angry outburst and a torrent of self-indulgent rudeness.

Nevertheless, guessing people's motives is not my business. My concern is to accept the healing Presence of God as the only energy ultimately in operation and to consciously recognize its wholeness as part of the situation. Simple. All I have to do is intone Love and stand back, and I'm trained to do that.

Still, when the angry person sits before me raging, sometimes it's pretty hard to remember that we're spiritual beings accepting a healing. Then I search my memory for the wonderful gift a good friend of mine gave me years ago. When this wise colleague found herself hardly loving someone hard to love, she would silently say, "God, I don't have it in me right now to love this person so please, do it through me."

What a perfect formula! Reminds me that it is God, after all, who does the loving and we the receiving of such love, angry or not.

In the faces of men and women I see God and in my own face in the glass; I find letters from God dropped in the street, and every one is signed by God's name.

Walt Whitman
The Enlightened Heart

Windows

IN MY PROFESSION AS A MINISTER I SOMETIMES FIND MYSELF privileged to be on hand for people who are dealing with a terminal illness. There may be a point in the course of the illness where they will approach the disease as something to be resisted mightily, and I stand with them in this attitude. But if they come to an inner acceptance that they will in fact experience physical death, sometimes the most magnificent opportunities for expansion become available to them. These I call "windows" because they seem to me to be clear openings through which the terminally ill begin to experience the largeness of their lives.

No longer concerned about the body's looks or their longevity, my friends begin to pay great attention to the vast spiritual networks within them and notice the trembling births of awareness that go on inside themselves, sometimes hour by hour. Most of us who are physically healthy are just too busy to notice these dawning illuminations, let alone search them out.

Buddhism suggests that death is an opportunity for growth, but this window is one many Westerners can barely imagine, so identified with our bodies are we. However, there comes a time when we know that our physical past is much greater than our physical future, and then, perhaps, the overlooked window will become more interesting. Certainly if we are at all curious our mind will want to know that we are more than a bundle of notions wrapped inside a body of flesh. Possibly all the love that has been circulating through us over time is moving toward some cosmic foreverness. What a window of exploration that could be!

Our contention is not that dead men live again, but that a living man never dies.

Ernest Holmes
The Science of Mind

To Spend or Not to Spend

AREN'T WE WONDERFULLY PARADOXICAL CREATURES, ESPE-cially when it comes to money? We think seriously about saving for a "nest egg," yet also long to treat ourselves to a languorous cruise. I suggest we ought to take a good look at both of these tendencies.

I get the chance to do so often, for my husband and I tend to operate from opposite ends of this spectrum. If, for instance, five hundred extra dollars should make its way to our mailbox, I would happily slip it into our savings account. My husband, on the other hand, would just as happily say, "Let's drive up to our favorite bed and breakfast!" These coaxial mindsets have often given us cause for head knocking, I can freely tell you; but they have also done something else, something far more valuable than any single decision about how to spend money.

These differences between us have made it necessary for both of us to really consider each other's fiscal values, which we might never have done had we been more alike. We have really had to acknowledge that the God Who Spends exists as well as the God Who Saves and to thoughtfully work to keep a loving balance between the two.

To spend or to save still comes up between us a lot and probably always will, since neither wants the other to give up being him or herself. But along with each instance comes the deeper gaze into what is really important for both of us...this time. Next time, we'll see...

We must first of all, then, perceive Spirit's purpose if we are to work with it. It can have but one self expression, but it may take many modes of activity.

Fenwicke Holmes
Being and Becomings

72

When Yesterday Becomes Today

WE NOW KNOW HOW TO EXTEND THE LIFE OF THE BODY, thanks to the advances of medical technology, but our spiritual technology is not yet so adept. Often we inhabit our body for longer and longer periods of time, while our mind seems almost to withdraw from the world of ideas and fall idle. How many of us have watched an older friend or family member cease to sparkle as some short circuit in the brain causes clarity of thought to recede into forgetfulness, often to be replaced by yesterday's memories, now made bright again as if given a second life. We who love them are saddened and confounded as we watch the changes in people we care about and now no longer know.

It is but a step away for us to wonder if we, too, may eventually reach back for yesterday's reveries as our old age approaches. We already know that we may, but we can also sharpen our spiritual techniques and practices to extend ourselves more completely into the ever-present freshness of the mind of God. I do believe that we can direct the thrust our mind shall take, whether it be toward the new surprises this day holds or the comfortable knowledge of yesterday.

It follows that we must begin to see ourselves as durable beings casting longer shadows upon our own mindscape. We'll have to adjust to our greater physical staying power and plan to be "sexy-generians" into expanded decades. We'll need to convince our body that we're still interested in today and tomorrow so our minds will not decide to curl up with yesterday.

If you take your mind to a level of functioning that is beyond age, then your body will begin to be touched by the same quality. It will age more slowly because your mind tells it to, at the deepest level. Seeing yourself as free from aging, you in fact will be.

Deepak Chopra
Perfect Health

On the Joyful Side

I, FOR ONE, HAVE NEVER BELIEVED THAT OUR RELIGIOUS OR spiritual beliefs should be morbid. We already know how to inflict pain upon ourselves and one another. Who needs a God who is even better at doing this? It seems that our tendency to cast God in the image and likeness of ourselves often causes us to give our deity all the qualities of whimsy that we possess, plus some real, cosmic clout to go along with it! It is as if we are determined to be punished for our lovelessness and ignorance, and so we've invented a God who is mean enough to do it!

Then why is it that something within us manages so often to bring forth a smile and even laughter? Perhaps the most natural of all our inner qualities is joy. Under very unlikely circumstances joy somehow surfaces—even during what would normally be our saddest times as human beings—when we attend funerals. Time after time, without trivializing the grief-filled cir-cumstance at all, some wonderful, humorous anecdote

75

remembered from the life of the one memorialized can lift the entire group with a burst of welcome laughter, even in the midst of sorrow.

What can this suggest except that joy is inescapable? It is the gift of our spiritual genetics, and it will heal us of all morbidities almost in spite of ourselves. This is the more likely cosmic sense, I feel, one which displays a God of mended hearts and lifted thoughts, the God that brings light into the dark places and spills wonder before all.

If I had my life to live over, I would start barefoot earlier in the spring and stay that way later in the fall. I would go to more dances. I would ride more merry-go-rounds. I would pick more daisies.

Nadine Stair, age 85

The Blooming Season

IN THE FRONT OF OUR HOUSE THERE ARE TWO CAMELLIA bushes that throw blossoms on the ground without cessation during the blooming season. Our home becomes filled with blooms throughout, and still we cannot keep up with the profusion of color. With almost obstinate consistency, the bushes seem bent on covering the ground beneath them with a profligacy of flowers. Then, once the flowering season is over, the two sit like happy green mounds awaiting the next round of color.

I, for one, am completely delighted with the joyful waste, and am again reminded of nature's seeming compulsion to express itself every chance it gets. Sidewalks, for instance, are no match for a healthy weed or a stray seed that seeks any small crack and bit of sun. I recall a single nasturtium seed which once made its way into a break in the concrete. It was certainly not coddled or nurtured, and still it grew into a two-foot bush riddled with brilliant flowers. There it stayed, pulling its nourishment from wherever it could, blooming through its season.

I am also reminded that I, too, am nature's own impulsion, replete with my own vigorous contribution of thoughts and actions, some of which manage to find recognizable expression, some of which fall to the side unutilized. I have but to stop for breath, and there within me is another season of ideas. At times I am concerned about the unused sumptuousness, but I would rather delight in all the beauties that make it into expression. Anyway, my season never ends. I'm a perennial.

Ultimately all things obey God's will.
All things come to equilibrium.

Carl Christensen
The Green Bible

Changes

MY LOVELY MOTHER ACHIEVED ONE OF HER GREATEST wishes. She lived to be 80 years old, almost 81, in fact. The last year of her life was difficult for her because she experienced so much physical pain, and also for us, her children, who felt ineffective in our attempts to help her. One bright morning her wise spirit understood that change was due, and she made a blessedly peaceful transition from the body which no longer served her vital energies.

I could not have wished anything less for her than the new estate that lay before her, and at the same time I had my own personal feelings of loss to deal with. This I understood and expected. My mother had been a cherished presence throughout my life, and suddenly the voice, the touch, the feel of that presence was gone. I had to readjust and to regear part of the emphasis of my life, and I also found myself a notch up on the mortality ladder. The last elder in our family had departed, and my generation had now assumed the role of elders.

This was a position I had not thought about before and I didn't quite know what to make of it.

My life changed entirely in just a moment, first through the wound of loss I felt because of my mother's transition and then through the rippling effect her departure had on my status in our family. Suddenly I became older than I thought I was, all because of the personal growth experience of a quiet little lady.

Every being in the universe is an expression of the Tao. It springs into existence, unconscious, perfect, free, takes on a physical body, lets circumstance complete it. That is why every being spontaneously honors the Tao.

Lao-tzu
The Enlightened Heart

80

The Undiscovered Country

ALONG WITH TREKKIES EVERYWHERE, I CATCH ALL THE *STAR Trek* movies and wait impatiently to see what Captain Kirk, Mr. Spock, and Dr. McCoy have in store for us each time, what unknown danger, what flight of fancy. My mind spins away as the Starship *Enterprise* soars into the light-laced heavens. Perhaps my greatest delight in these fantastic adventures lies in the inner contemplations they foster in me as they traverse the far reaches of outer space.

In one of these adventures a major character spoke of peace as being an undiscovered country, and my internal circuits went into orbit. Had I ever really lived in the country called peace? Many times peace is an unknown to us, a place we'd like to visit but cannot really imagine ourselves inhabiting consistently. Consider what we might have to give up to live in the country called peace! We might not be able always to be right. We might have to consider another's good along with our own. We might have to cease defending

81

our flanks in order to know what it is to feel—and accept—vulnerability. We might have to expand the borders of the known status quo to include the hitherto unknown and unconsidered dreams of others.

We are entering a great time of exploring our inner space to discover a longed-for sense of well being, which each of us can then carry out into the world. The trek we have to take may indeed seem daunting but it is leading us to our spiritual home ground. It is a place to boldly go where we may not have gone before.

Fear does not need to keep us from a wanted result. Managing ourselves in relationship to fear makes it possible for us also to manage our relationship to all barriers and obstacles to the result.

Douglas Yeaman and Noel McInnis
The Power of Commitment

The Little Pearls

CAN YOU REMEMBER A DAY WHEN YOU WERE DEEPLY DIS-
couraged because nothing seemed to be going right?
The check did not come in the mail, the person with
whom you had an appointment didn't show up, and
you got out of bed that morning with a beaut of a
headache! Then out of the blue a call came from someone who seemed to know you needed to hear something soothing, and the gentle words spoken were just
exactly right somehow. Amazing! And this happens
often, I find. In fact I have now begun to make room for
what I call "the little pearls"—the calls, the notes, the
kindnesses that come when I seem to need them most.

I suppose I really shouldn't find this amazing at all
but rather quite natural and timely considering the
scope of our spiritual existence. If, as I believe, we live
a universal life and the cosmic Spirit dances in our
hearts, certainly it knows what we need and how to
please us. If we have set ourselves to the fullness of living and consciously anticipate joy in our lives, will we

not send signals to our greater Spirit to supply these things? Even through the mists of forgetfulness, then, our dancing Spirit has the message and knows how to make fullness and joy appear to us. I think the ever giving Spirit lies in wait, patiently offering its gifts to the awakened soul and to the half-asleep mind as well, and when the big goodies can't get through the fog, the small ones slip through the cracks.

Hence, the little pearls.

It is love that asks, that seeks, that knocks, that finds, and that is faithful to what it finds.

St. Augustine
1000 Inspirational Things

The Pit

Black vistas,
No light…no light anywhere,
Even the sun's expanse does not crack through
  the hardness of my darkened heart.
So sunk into unknowing am I.
Such is my mindscape today.
Overloaded with morbidities and reflections on
  past failures,
The pain in my mind so great that it takes
  hostage my unpained body.
I move and go nowhere.
I think and know nothing.
My feelings sear my soul with anxious fire.
Will I ever be myself again?

Thanks to my God for the cool flame of Being
  which burns the dross without harm to me.
Thanks to my God who sees through me
  when I cannot see.
Thanks to my God.

Playing the Game

WE HAVE ALL HEARD THE OLD BROMIDE, "IT ISN'T WHETHER you win or lose, it's how you play the game." This little axiom is lodged in my memory, seldom brought to consciousness except when something comes along to remind me of it, and recently something did.

It was the time for the Olympic Games, and I had settled in to watch, as I always do. I enjoy seeing superb athletes engaged in their sports. To me they're all winners, all worthy disciples of their practices. What do I care if someone is off a tenth of a second? I love watching them all fly and twirl through their paces.

As I watched I became aware that those who seemed to possess the greatest joy were those *not* in medal contention. They seemed thrilled to simply participate, to give their sport all they could without concern for winning or losing, just doing their best. If a medal showed up, wonderful outcome! If not, wonderful anyway.

Those in medal contention seemed to find little pleasure in their performances. Winning was everything, and God forbid that anyone should slip or fall! Literally hounded by the media, these favored had little quiet time to mentally consider what was truly important to them.

As I watched a favored one see the gold slip away by a fraction of a second, I saw a glorious performance suddenly viewed as wanting, and the old bromide took on new meaning for me as it leapt to the forefront of my mind. The heart's joyful participation in the game is what matters. How sad that we have made winning the only important outcome.

There is a place that you are to fill and no one else can fill, something you are to do, which no one else can do.

Plato

The Child

AS I LOOKED INTO THE EYES OF MY NEWEST GRANDCHILD I had to wonder: is she as young as she looks? What a question, some might wonder. Here this pink and white bit of humanity lay in my arms, barely hours old, and this silly grandmother is already concerned about her age!

This query is not as facetious as it seems. Some there are who would nod their heads knowingly, cast their gaze into the heavens, and consider what an old soul she no doubt is. Whether or not one believes in reincarnation, I think we are contemplating the timelessness of life itself whenever we look into the eyes of a newborn. We are confused, I think, by the ephemeral nature of our bodies and consistently mistake them for ourselves. We think we come into existence and then cease to exist, just as our bodies do, and thereby incorrectly estimate the infinitude in which we are enveloped.

As I looked at this small, soft face squinting at me, I know I began to spot the genes that had formed her already majestic history. I saw her mother's body, her father's skin, and as she grows I knew I'd see the gestures of grandparents and great-grandparents in her movements. I'd listen to her speak and hear her make statements as a child that I myself did not comprehend until my adulthood. Everything I am and know, I bequeathed to her as well as all the bequests given to me as I emerged from the Soul of eternity. My heart and hers are part of Its heart.

This girl is old—but we won't reveal her age just yet. In her own good time she'll tell us.

All the flowers of all the tomorrows are in the seeds of today.

Evelyn Beecher
Beecher's Features

Perfect Does As Perfect Is

MUCH PRAYER WORK IS DONE BASED ON THE PREMISE OF perfection. The one doing the praying affirms that that which is absolutely right is taking place even as the prayer is being spoken, a kind of acknowledgment that the ground from which all things issue forth is inherently perfect. Intellectually this thinking makes sense if anything is to be healed or renewed at all since there must be an untarnished beginning from which to refer. The blueprint in the mind of the Builder must be complete.

Seeing or identifying something as being perfect is quite another matter, for now we get into the world of perceptions, and one man's meat certainly can be another man's poison! Darned if I can tell you what perfection looks like, but I do know how it feels. What I do know is that perfection is not so much a thing of matter as it is a thing of consciousness.

Now and a very occasional then, I have had the complete joy of participating in a circumstance which falls together—perfectly. It could not have been planned or foreseen, because it really does serendipitously fall together. Every person, every surrounding is somehow effortlessly exactly right for the experience, and it is far larger than the sum of all the participants. Once the participants disperse, it cannot be replicated. The perfection must come again another day when once again all things fall together.

What stays with each one involved in such an experience is the unmistakable ring of what has taken place. Everything that needed to come to pass did come to pass, and the memory of this cannot be forgotten.

The very key to spiritual mind healing is a consciousness that we are living in a spiritual universe now, a living universe now, and that there is no difference between mind and what mind does.

Ernest Holmes
The Anatomy of Healing Prayer

My Heart Sings God's Music

I BELIEVE MYSELF TO BE ONE OF GOD'S DIVINE MUSICIANS. I may not have the extraordinary vocal talents of Kathleen Battle, but my music interprets itself through my brain and runs out through my fingertips into the written word. My mind sings and sings with ideas that make their way into print.

Not many of us have the resonant tones of Pavarotti but we can sing God's music through the actions of our lives. I have felt the lyricism in a piece of sculpture. I have seen the harmonies in a Kashmiri prayer rug. I have heard the finely tuned artistry in a newly rebuilt engine. Nor does something require a long process of maturation to be considered art, for I have seen the bright and joyous flowing forth of bold colors in the works of children as well.

I guess what I'm saying is that I believe all of God's creations to be resident artists. The flora and fauna of Nature don't shrink from complete expression. They are always entirely what they were designed to be. Human beings, on the other hand, often struggle with something called self-esteem and frequently seem not to know of their inherent artistry.

Is the risk of being beautiful and doing beautifully so great that we are hesitant to extend ourselves? Is our predilection to competition so strong that there can be only a few magnificent ones, all others deemed not noteworthy? I cannot believe this even for a moment. I hear, see, and feel much too much beautiful music everywhere I go.

Not "Revelation" 'tis that waits,
But our unburnished eyes—

Emily Dickinson
The Enlightened Heart

After I'm Gone

LOOKING AT TIME ON A LARGE SCALE, I KNOW THAT MY LITtle physical life is, by comparison to infinity, about the length of a snap of the fingers. Still, it's mine, and I'm plugging along doing the best I can with it. Some days I catch myself coming and going with my grand accomplishments. Other days I wonder whether or not I can do much of anything right, both of which attitudes I suspect are fairly normal.

In the midst of it all sometimes I can't help but wonder what difference any of this will make after I'm gone. I trust my children and grandchildren will have felt my influence, and maybe even some great-grandchildren, if I'm lucky. Perhaps there will be a few other groups of people who might give importance to my having been in their lives, but in a few finger snaps all these folks will be gone too, and memories of me along with them.

One could get really depressed over stuff like this, but I don't, because there is something in me that feels a bigger scene is being played out, and I'm one of the players. I can't begin to imagine all the parts I may be playing, but I know I'm in the game. And aren't we all? Aren't we all some of the puzzle pieces in the great Unity? Don't we know we have no duplicates even if we do have look-alikes, and don't our nonduplicatable selves make a nest in ultimate Reality?

I believe so, and therefore I can't get too mopey about my too-short physical span. I know I'll be here—even after I'm gone.

We need fear nothing in the Universe. We need not be afraid of God. We may be certain that all will arrive at the fine goal, that not one will be missing.

Ernest Holmes
The Science of Mind

What Color Is My Soul?

THE *ISMS* IN OUR LAND BECOME TEDIOUS TO ME—RACISM, sexism, elitism, and so forth. Do I stand before God as a white female, an American? When my body is slipped from me, will my light present itself as a minister of metaphysics? When the wave drops back into the ocean, will the ocean view it as an especially wonderful, distinctive thing, or will it simply welcome it as part of itself?

I believe that we waves glorify the great Ocean of Life with our unique antics, but that we are equalized when we drop back in to discover that our samenesses far outnumber our uniquenesses. The Bible suggested that we have many inventions, and we surely have invented all the notions about who is better, more beautiful, more creative, more worthwhile. This, no doubt, is because we still are so unaware of that which Ernest Holmes called Soul Stuff that binds us into Oneness.

I was raised to think in terms of separateness and

otherness, which was what we understood at that time. My mind knows better now, but sometimes the old habits return and the old judgments begin to appear. But those judgments won't run me...not if I don't want them to.

My three sisters are beautiful and ethnically diverse. We chose each other because we love each other and because we all possess the great equalizer...many samenesses. We laugh together, we weep together, we melt into the same God together, and we worry together also. We worry that it may take a long time for all people to know that all souls are colorless and that all hearts throb to one universal Pulse.

In the cherry blossom's shade
there's no such thing
as a stranger.

Issa
The Enlightened Heart

Let Go and Let God

ONE OF THE MOST DURABLE, INSPIRATIONAL AXIOMS ON hand for our consideration for many years has been this little powerhouse: Let go and let God. What a wonderful guideline! What a clear, simple, no-fail way to think, and something that believers in spiritual principles espouse with glee. If the great Truth is that the mind of God is the mind we are using every time we think, why not just let go of our opinions and trust that God always knows perfect resolution?

Why not, indeed! What we may not have always considered through this simple approach is that we are not usually willing to be the simple beings that it would take to "let go and let God." We have a vested interest in circumstances turning out in certain ways. The truth as we are willing to accept it is very often the truth that follows the lines of our desires and beliefs. I have known those who truly could let go and let God, often because some difficult circumstance had literally stripped them of any resistance they may have had.

Driven to their knees, all posturing burned to ashes, there was no other place to turn but to God. But this is so traumatic and costly in wear and tear. One wonders if we could not more easily decide upon this course in our own good time.

The greatest complication is the uncomplicating of our opinion-laden beliefs and the striding into simple acceptance that God is being God at all times. Nothing changes this. When and if we can come to this simplicity, we can let go and let God, and do so with real joy.

You have a sense of living in nested realities. You are at once an atom, a molecule, a cell, an organism, a body, a soul, a beloved within the mind of God.

Jean Houston
The Search for the Beloved

Memories

It has been said that our memories tend to make up a part of our self-image, and there is great wisdom in this statement. Within each of us resides a cellar of time, a great repository wherein all the events of our lives are stored, waiting for us to bring them forth for reference; and if they truly be for reference, we are recognizing them wisely. If, however, we are perceiving these memories as the baseline of our existence, we are giving them far more power than they deserve.

Our memories can give us clues as to how we have done things in the past, handy references as to what we may wish to change if we will use them accordingly. When we mix ourselves up with our memories, though, we sometimes begin to think that these remembrances are what we are, and they cannot be. They are done deals, and we are living potentials.

I referred to our well of memories as residing in a cellar of sorts. Is it not so that houses with cellars are firmly planted in the deep, rich earth which enfolds them and supports them? The house and its cellar must have the security of the earth to maintain their solidarity. We, too, are kinds of housings, deep and varied, which reside in our own sphere of cosmic wholeness. Our hopes and our aspirations, as well as our memories, are secured in this greater richness of being. Therefore our strength and ongoingness are in the greater being, not in the memories. On our next trip down memory lane, let's remember this image.

The distant shores of silences begin
at the door. You cannot fly there
like a bird. You must stop, look deeper,
still deeper, until nothing deflects the soul
from the deepmost deep!

Karol Wojtyla
Collected Poems

When Heroes Fall

TO SOME OF OUR BRIGHTEST AND MOST TALENTED PEOPLE, we seem to ascribe almost magical qualities. They become larger than life, possessors of skills and beauty seemingly denied the average person, and so we often come to live a portion of our hopes and dreams through them. We lift them upward and make silent demands: Be perfect. Be beautiful forever. Never have warts. Above all, don't disappoint me.

But sometimes they do disappoint us. Along with their beauty and talent they carry the same shadowy insecurities that we carry, and now and again these sorry sides burst forth with a bang. Our heros are then hurled from Valhalla, and we see that they are what we are, human beings trying to make their way in a complicated world. We do not want to forgive them this ordinariness, this seeming less-ness, and just as we loved them we begin to hate them for being flawed.

What are we doing to our heroes and to ourselves? Are we asking others to lend life to us by endowing them with superhuman traits? Do we really believe that Superman does exist, waiting in the nearest telephone booth for the opportunity to fly forth to make all things well?

The heroic man and woman are not some of us but all of us. They are the best of beings which lie within each. There is strength to be called upon, love to be shown, wisdom and courage to be discovered when we strive to do the best that we know to do. These aspirations are not unrealistic. They are found in real people...you and me. The hero lives in us. We do not have to reflect someone else's light.

No, I don't merely want to be just. I stand on a threshold, glimpse a new world.

Karol Wojtyla
Collected Poems

Our Flight

In the warm wings of my knowing,
I rise up.
I seem clear,
But I'm struggling.

What holds me back?
I have already cast light on my dimness.
What else holds me—or who?

Hands are grasping at me
And voices cry to me.
They are the hands and voices of others,
And yet they are mine as well.

I believed I could move on alone.
But perhaps I cannot.
The hands and voices
Which are mine and not mine
Must rise up with me.

One Life, One Voice, One Mind, One Flight.

Power

POWER. WE ALL WANT IT, ALTHOUGH SOME OF US ARE afraid of it. We think that other people can give it or take it. What little we feel we do have, we often try to give away, and there are always those who are more than willing to believe they can take it from us.

What exactly is this so-desired power? Is it something we can lay our hands on? Money and possessions, perhaps? Is it command over others from a vaunted place? Princes, principalities, things present, things to come? Maybe. Are these things power, or are they simply some of the outer forms that power can take, in which case they are not power at all, since all are perishable? Money and possessions cannot go with us as our bodies molder in the grave. Princes and principalities disappear with time. Things present and even things to come eventually become things that were. Power these things are not. Loaded with power they are.

No one can give me what the Almighty has given me, nor can I ever get rid of it, no matter how decidedly I may try. My power energizes my beliefs, whatever they may be. My power lends life to my relationships and height to my aspirations. It quivers in my quickened heartbeats when I am fearful, and it will fly with me to my next destination when I quit my body.

In the book of Romans (8:31) the apostle Paul said, "If God is for us, who is against us?" Who, indeed, except the shadowy arm of our own ignorance which seems to withhold that which cannot be withheld! Not for long. Paul also said, "Now I know in part; then I shall understand fully, even as I have been fully understood." (I Corinthians 13:12)

Do you not know that you are God's Temple and that God's Spirit dwells in you?

I Corinthians 3:16 RSV

When There Is Only God

THE SPIRITUALLY INTROSPECTIVE AMONG US LIKE TO SAY that God is all there is, that God created form and void out of its own Essence and imbued all with life, intelligence, maleness, and femaleness, and keeps the whole thing rolling according to the creative process inherent within the nature of God itself. We all love this idea and contemplate it vigorously. We write books about it, create prayers using it, and hold conventions to discuss it. We split hairs over it, rigorously de-gender it, and religiously turn away from the world of effects so that we may understand it more clearly.

But what happens on the days that there *really* is only God, when nothing is going the way it should, when all our spiritual stalwarts are somewhere else and when the usually facile words come haltingly to our lips because our thoughts find no resting place? Yes...well, maybe the God that is who we are is the grounding place that our unsure feet seek.

I know this disconnected feeling; indeed, have

known it many times even as one steeped in spiritual practice. My feet still sink in unsureness from time to time, but my God never fails me. There is no depth to which I may fall where God cannot reach me. It is the depth as well as the height. No matter what, I always touch the ground of my being which awaits me with quiet love. It sweeps through every jumble of my mind, through every separated thought, and trickles through my very pores if I but invite it. I never know just when or quite how the unreasoned knowing will fill me with its passion for me, but it always does.

I know there really is only God.

When you have reached a new and higher place of spiritual awareness, remember that with it comes the challenge to abide there...Your work is to guard it, like country newly won, so that it will not be retaken by the enemies—within yourself.

Letters of the Scattered Brotherhood

Watching the Fish

ONE LAZY, SUNNY AFTERNOON I SAT WATCHING THE SMALL school of koi and goldfish in our meticulously-kept little backyard pond. "God! Are they beautiful!" I thought to myself. Lucky, too. They don't have any career concerns. They don't have to worry about pleasing a congregation or satisfying a Board of Trustees. And they've got no natural enemies. We've seen to that with a mesh cover to keep the cats and the raccoons out at night. They probably eat better than we do, too...plenty of algae and the nutritionally balanced food we give them. With any luck at all, the koi among them will outlive us!

As I sat in this reverie a single word floated to the surface of my thoughts...doorkeeper. "Doorkeeper?" I questioned aloud, and then slowly, I remembered the words from Psalm 84, words I hadn't thought about in years. "I had rather be a doorkeeper in the house of my God, than to dwell in the tents of wickedness."

A little dawn began to break, and I patted myself

with my very non-finlike hands and smiled. While the pond can hardly be called a "tent of wickedness," it is a tent of sorts and one my finny friends can't leave. I, of course, can go wherever my feet will take me, and I can hie myself to the house of my God wherever I find it. Would I really want to exchange what I know and what I am for such watery pleasantries? I knew the answer as I sat in silence gazing at the fish frolics. Shining bodies knifing through the waters; they probably don't even know they're beautiful.

How, then, shall I live?
To celebrate with plantings,
And to give thanks, always.
That we may know ourselves
By the fruit we bear.

Carl Christensen
The Green Bible

Living with Diversity Is Difficult

I HAVE TO SAY IT: LIVING WITH DIVERSITY IS HARD. IT'S DIFFI-cult. I love to think of myself as open-minded and flexible, and I wish this were honestly true. Once I thought it was, but now I know it's not. What is true is that I'm not kidding myself anymore, and what's also true is that I am at least really willing to entertain the discomfort of diversity.

I'm willing to eat strange foods, not just look at them and wrinkle my nose. I'm willing to listen to different music, not just examine the CD jackets with curiosity. And I'm willing to stay in the game called "Playing for Keeps."

Once it was fairly easy to pick up my marbles and go home when strange folks began to say their say and do their thing. Now I find it unwholesome to leave. It's too painful, too hurtful, too dangerous. Equanimity is alive and well but only among those who are willing to test its waters. When I leave, I've lost. Actually all have lost because ground and time have been ceded to the path of least resistance, and I find I only have to start all over again. We all must.

There is a sweetness of being that underlies all the rough edges, and every now and again it will suddenly surface in effortless harmony in the midst of huge differences, bringing peace on its wings. I wish it could remain present forever, but it doesn't. Sooner or later diversity kicks in, and we're off in our corners again.

Sweetness, come stay.
I'll let go my ego
In order to play
In the game we are living,
Forgiven, forgiving.
All for the new face I'm seeing today.

Transformation Is an Inside Job

ONE OF THE LOVELIEST "WARM FUZZIES" MAKING THE
rounds today is the concept of transformation. Trans-
for-ma-tion, four whole syllables which mean the
changing of shape, and the changing of shape suggests
an entire reworking of the means by which shape
comes about. This is big stuff, and it is not for sissies.
Transformation is hard work, dear and costly, for it
means that the familiar ruts in our brains have to be
discarded in favor of new ones.

Ultimately, transformation cannot be looked on as a
warm fuzzy at all, but more of a hot crucible burning
away the dross of dull perceptions so that only the
clarity of self-knowing remains. Actually, being transformed is part of our destiny, only our new shapes
require our openness and receptivity rather than the
pursuit of goals—being and becoming rather than getting. In the being and becoming, that which we want to
get is drawn to us automatically.

There is a small glitch in this mighty concept, for new

shapes can only come from newly discovered *internal* vistas. It is vistas which attract our desires, and we do not want to look at our internal landscapes. We want to be transformed from the outside in, very much like an electorate which wants a newly created government to make everything right without interfering with its own special interests.

We cannot have it both ways. The transforming Spirit does not give something for nothing. But with our earnest efforts, it gives magnificently, more than we could imagine. It transforms.

> *Take your practical powers and stretch them out*
> *Until they span the chasm between contradictions...*
> *for the god wants to know himself in you.*

Rainer Maria Rilke
The Enlightened Heart

Ideas Reside in My Mind

ONE OF THE THINGS FOR WHICH I SEEM TO HAVE A NATURAL talent is the gathering of ideas. In a way I feel like the man driving a harvester through a mature wheat field. The harvester cuts down the golden stalks, and they lie on the ground, waiting to be bundled up. I simply bundle them up and give them a place to go.

As far as I am concerned, ideas are always waving their heads at me. If I'm asleep to them, I miss them, but when I open my eyes, they are waiting. People have often asked me where my ideas come from, and I have mentioned the various articles I may have seen or an occasional comment I may have heard. I now know that the ideas have been in my mind all the time. Perhaps some picture or story activated thoughts in a certain area, but the corresponding ideas, once stimulated, literally stream through my brain currents into my pen and onto the paper.

I know they preexist before I capture them because I can essentially see them dancing before me, almost as a form of seduction, since I cannot resist them. Once an idea finds me it will not let me go until I scratch down a few notes.

This little bit of creativity is perhaps the most exciting thing that ever happens to me. Bungee jumping and fire walking can never hold the thrill for me that idea stalking does...almost like a birth of sorts, since I'm never sure what the finished product will look like until it appears. Love in bloom, I guess.

The idea is father to the fact.

Ernest Holmes
The Science of Mind

To Me I Sing

REGULAR DOSES OF MUSIC, THAT'S WHAT WE NEED! Regular intervals of self celebrations, of singing to ourselves in recognition of the Spirit of God which lives within us! I am not talking about whistling in the dark to keep our spirits up. I am talking about keeping before us the remembrance that we are the lighted ways wherein God is being revealed. I already know that no one can provide our light for us because I've tried riding on the coattails of other people's inspirations. They soared ahead, and I fell by the wayside.

We contain our own inspiration, and at the same time we've got to keep it percolating through our own energies. There are simply too many sensationalized images put before us which tend to keep us unsettled; and the more unsettled we let ourselves become, the more off track and uninspired we become.

Hymns of praises bellowed forth in the shower, songs of love quietly crooned, hummed smiles as we walk from place to place, these are intimate intonations from the God Self within us to the God Beings that we present to the outer world every day. Let's strike up the music that thrills our souls or create little lyrics of our own; and if we forget the words, some well-placed "la's" will do. It's the celebratory spirit that counts.

I believe the Spirit of God in us loves our music—rousing marching songs, love songs, songs of sacred honor, songs to dance to, rhythms to tap to, the brightening trill of the universe itself.

Strike up the band! Bring out the chorus! Sing for the health of our own souls!

I celebrate myself, and sing myself,
and what I assume you shall assume,
For every atom belonging to me
as good belongs to you.

Walt Whitman
Leaves of Grass

Disaster's Gold

HAVING BEEN ON HAND FOR THE DEVASTATING EARTHQUAKE and firestorm in the San Francisco-Oakland area, I can easily recall the newspaper and TV stories of ordinary people engaging in extraordinary acts—pulling people from wreckage, risking their lives to assist strangers. This is not an uncommon story. We read many of them whenever disaster strikes, and each time I ask myself, Why does it take disaster to bring the human family together? Why can't we act like kin all the time?

I don't know. Maybe it takes extraordinary demands for us to become extraordinary people. Maybe it's just too easy to become careless toward one another unless our feet are to the fire. I'm guilty of this myself, I know. My own concerns seem foremost in my mind until something of much greater urgency causes me to set them aside for the time being.

Perhaps I ought to be somewhat mollified in knowing that I have it in me to rise to the necessities of the occasion, but I'm still thinking, "Why must it take an occasion?" Perhaps if enough of us are asking this same question we may decide to do away with the need for the occasion and take on a little of Mother Teresa's attitude of love for its own sake. Surely we can't lose. We can be enlarged only through the extension of ourselves; and we're not talking here about heroism. We're talking about participating in the human family because we choose to.

There's gold here—not money perhaps, but depth and genuineness and shared living—not mined from disaster's tears.

Gold does not lie in shining
nuggets on the ground.
We first remove the sod
that covers it
and draw the pure metal from
the dross that holds it.

Margaret Stortz
Flights into Life

The Older I Grow, the Younger I Become

THE OLDER I GROW, THE YOUNGER I BECOME. THIS BEMUS-
ing statement has crossed my mind off and on for several years now, possibly because my shortening physical life and my lengthening spiritual life are teaching
me a thing called perspective. For instance, I no longer
believe that I do my thinking in a physical vacuum,
alone and unique in my fears and aspirations. I believe
now that I do more than move through time, watching
my body lose its post-adolescent look, wondering how
self-affirming a face-lift would be. I believe I am moving through the eddies and nuances of life itself, clus-
tered with others who are doing the same thing—
maybe becoming younger too.

I invented my old age when I was a kid; I was so
serious, so concerned about doing the right things.
Now I am reinventing my youth as I discover some of
the changeless parts of myself. I have gone through
sickness, loss of dreams, the deaths of loved ones, and
I have discovered that none of these things diminished

123

me, not as I thought they would. Perhaps I am touching a cosmic durability that is defanging my fears of physical mortality. Perhaps I am finally beginning to discover what is important and what is not. I'd like to think so.

The warm sun, my loved one's smile, my genuine acceptance of my talents, the ability to say no to what is not mine to do—these are some of the appreciations of my increasingly youthful state. Years ago, I was just too old to notice them.

To insist on one's place in the scheme of things
and to live up to that place,
To empower others in their reaching for some place
in the scheme of things,
To do these things is to make fairy tales come true.

Robert Fulghum
Uh-Oh

Why Do We Pray?

WHY DO WE PRAY? THIS MAY SEEM A BIZARRE QUESTION TO ask, especially when it comes from a person who considers herself spiritually aware. Nevertheless, I ask it, since prayer is one of the greatest of all spiritual tools, the one thing all religions use in common. I long to know what moves us to a prayerful stance.

Is it the point of last resort, the seemingly futile attempt to solve a problem when we've tried everything else? Is it used as a means of barter, with the hope of enticing a whimsical God into giving us tit for tat? Is prayer beseeching a discriminating God who may deem our prayer worthy of consideration—if we have the proper belief system?

I suspect that all of these reasons are so, and how sad if they are the only reasons. Prayer is so much more, especially when used with real awareness. Prayer is at the very least the consciously opened door to Divine Connection. When we pray, we know it! There is no mistaking the prayerful intention, whether it be conducted as a hysterical last resort or part of a beloved, consistent spiritual practice.

Does God hear prayers? Of course, if hearing is considered the universal ability to respond. Does God answer prayers? Of course. If philosopher Ernest Holmes is correct in his comment that the answer to prayer is in the prayer itself, then our very thoughts already begin to form the outcomes.

Are we ready for answered prayer? Good question. Since we are so often concerned about God's response to us, we might ask whether or not we are open to the response.

Our words along the nature of our faith make our faith a working principle.

Emma Curtis Hopkins
Scientific Christian Mental Practice

My Busy Body

UP UNTIL RECENTLY, I WOULD NOT CUT MY BODY ANY SLACK. I would expect it to go on under my demands without complaint or surcease. Not that I would ask this of my car, not at all! I see that my car is serviced regularly. My body, however, I considered quite a different matter.

Somehow I guess I felt that my bit of flesh and blood was really not a part of me, something loaned perhaps, something so temporal that it did not merit my consideration. It had no voice to tell me otherwise, no voice, that is, that I was paying attention to...until the day that I wound up flat on my back with a pinched nerve. This I noticed since the pain was exquisitely real. I knew my body was speaking to me!

Pain is a very effective messenger, as I suspect the reader may have noticed at different times; and when the body becomes frustrated in its gentle attempts to get our attention, it begins to malfunction. Pain takes over, telling us we have neglected the physical form in which our spirit dwells on its journey through life. The body needed rest, and so it put me in a position which made resting the only thing I was able to do.

I'm looking back on the episode now, and I really do trust that I have grown up enough to realize that balanced living is something to be not only sought after, but treasured. The term "mind/body being" has real meaning for me now, and I plan to treat my physical self with humility from now on. I've learned how to listen.

The physical body is evolved for the purpose of allowing consciousness to function on this plane. The body is necessary to this plane, since only through a physical body can we properly function here.

Ernest Holmes
The Science of Mind

Thanks for Every Little Thing

MUCH HAS BEEN SAID BY THE SPIRITUALLY-MINDED ABOUT giving thanks at every opportunity, no matter how difficult. For a long time this practice seemed like so much metaphysical "make nice" to me, almost like trying to deny that there was something to be concerned about. I found that I was dead wrong about this, that giving consistent, effortless thanks in no way diminishes the need for handling situations but rather paves the way for doing so with a lighter heart.

When I was flat on my back with a persistent muscle spasm I didn't think I had much to feel thankful for at the time. I really did know the efficacy of giving thanks for every little thing, but hadn't done so for a while. It was a good time to test an old axiom, and so I did. I gave thanks that the sun came out early on my birthday, which was unusual for the time of year. I gave thanks that I could bend over enough to put my socks on by myself. Ridiculous little stuff! But it started working. I noticed that I could lift my pain-filled body around a lot more easily because I had already lifted my thoughts. I noticed that, at least on that particular day, I never did fall back into the dour state in which I had awakened, and little sweet surprises rained on me off and on the whole day.

Will giving thanks for little things change the world's mighty events? Maybe not, but it can help me change my mind about a sorry situation.

I have found that what we do is transcend our experiences, not go up and come right back down in them.

George Bendall
Collected Essays of George Bendall

In My Solitude

I REMEMBER A WONDERFUL, LUSH, MOURNFUL OLD SONG BY the name of "In My Solitude" which evoked lots of pain, sorrow, and loneliness. It was the kind of song that could fill you with a deep river of tears and cause every lost romance to spring forth as if it had happened only yesterday. It was a great song! Misery in melody!

One line of the song went, "In my solitude, you haunt me." What a straight-on perception! In our solitude, when there's nothing to do but let our minds drift, everything haunts us—not just the "you's" in our lives but the "what's" and the "why not's" and the "why me's." It's a real paradox to me how so much activity can be going on when it's so quiet!

Recently, I decided I wanted my solitude to be a real solace rather than a launching pad for pain and agony blast-offs. I knew my God Self was lying in wait for me anyway just trying to get a crack at me, so I invited it in. I settled down. I made an effort not to be seduced by the usual internal conversation, and I became—

quiet. It was rich. I was silent but I was full. Nothing was happening, and everything was happening. Oh, it does take effort at times to defang the subconsciousness beasties, but I have a silent destination now. In my solitude, nothing haunts me anymore. Nothing comes to get me that I cannot dissipate in my quiet.

Funny what old songs can teach us.

The world is no more than the Beloved's single face;
In the desire of the One to know its own beauty, we exist.

Ghalib
The Enlightened Heart

132

The Vietnam Memorial

Black marble angles,
Cold stone, alive with bequeathed memories.
America's wailing wall commands the oncomer
With agonizing vitality none can mistake.

Hands gently fingering etched names,
Tears silently disappearing into whiskery faces.
The comers stand quietly, their thoughts unrevealed
  to one another.

Those seeking names drive their private pain
Deeply into the black remembrance.
Those with no names reel unsteadily,
Made almost giddy with invisible anguish
Shot from the columns of memorialized humanity.

Can this history ever be bound up?
Can the unforgiveness and irresolution rise
  into some form of wholeness?

Endless, drooping bouquets adorn the walls.
Endless...new ones every day.
Perhaps they know the answer.

Five Blind Men

AND THE STORY GOES:

Five blind men were trying to describe an elephant. One, holding its leg, said, "The elephant is like a great tree." Another grasped one its ears and cried, "Ah, but the elephant is like a palm frond." A third held the elephant's tail and said, "No, the elephant is like a great rope." The fourth fingered the elephant's tusk and responded, "It is hard, smooth, and strong," while the last man, feeling the great trunk, said, "You're all wrong. The elephant is like a large, coiling snake."

Now I'm the sort of person who has a "morning after" mentality. When I go to the movies, I try to imagine what might happen down the road after the movie is finished. Will the lovebirds, for instance, still be speaking to one another in another year? With regard to our elephant story, I can imagine the animal shifting its position a quarter turn, thus giving each man another part to examine. Since all the men were so positive they knew all about the beast, how undone would they become?

I guess I'm suggesting that we, as Truth seekers, are a bit like the blind men. We're so sure our little corner of the Truth is the accurate description. What would happen to us if the beast moved a bit? Could we stand the shock of not being completely right? Might be we should consider our view of Truth like a butterfly and hold it very lightly in our hands, lest the need come for it to take wing and fly away.

Take your practiced powers and stretch them out until they span the chasm between two contradictions...For the god wants to know himself in you.

Rainer Maria Rilke
The Enlightened Heart

Am I Getting Old?

I THINK THERE IS A PLACE BETWEEN YOUTH AND OLD AGE where the ice gets pretty thin at times. Sometimes we feel on solid ground, everything well in hand; and other times it gets a little dicey out there. Things don't seem to click into place as sharply, and our body doesn't help much. There are definitely some mornings when I wonder about the face that looks back at me in the mirror. Is it really taking longer to look the way I used to look, or am I just imagining things? Am I approaching 100 years old, or does it just feel that way? If I could *see* my gray hairs, how many of them would there be?

But then, these feelings move on, and I find myself seizing upon an idea with all the gusto and freshness of a five-year-old. My mind snaps into place with all the finesse of one skilled at living and calls forth the wisdom of the ages in a twinkling.

My eyes tell me that part of me is getting older, but my mind remembers that part of me is ageless; and while my physical connections get a bit frayed around the edges, my cosmic conduit is river-clear and in motion, even as I sleep. I can't get terminally morbid over some encroaching wrinkles. What I know runs so deep and sweet that it lends an occasional lightness to my step and always a blessed, blessed assurance of my never-diminishing being.

The time and place of a man's life on earth are the time and place of his body, but the meaning and significance of his life are as vast and far-reaching as his gifts, his times, and the passionate commitment of all his powers can make it.

Howard Thurman
With Head and Heart

Making Changes

OH, HOW WE'RE ALL UP FOR CHANGE THESE DAYS! WE SAY we've got to approach ourselves and other people in new ways. We've got to let go of old attitudes so we can see the world from a whole fresh viewpoint. We all know this, so we import books on change making to have models to follow. We take workshops and seminars by the zillions to get trained in the art of becoming a new person, a loving person, a forgiving and non-judgmental person. Sometimes, though, being an agent for change is no fun, especially when I've got a big, fat judgment that I'm planning to molder in a while. I do love my old habits.

It's time, though, and, truthfully, past time to recognize that win/lose setups do not ultimately benefit anyone. By now we must know inwardly, at some quiet level, that if we don't all win, no one wins. Still, our mindsets suggest that wars can produce victors, that we must deal with others from an adversarial stance, and that life must be hard. We have been closed and cavalier to those people who seem different from us and we are even sometimes downright wretched toward them. Since we held all the marbles, why not?

Suppose God *is* our cosmic parent? We then are somehow all related and somehow all members of a universal spiritual community. No church or belief system is first in line. In life's family, we are not "only children." This is no longer a time for spoiled brats. It's time for healthy, global neighborhoods.

I feel that the essence of all spiritual life is your emotion, your attitude toward others. Once you have pure and sincere motivation, all the rest follows.

The Dalai Lama
Ocean of Wisdom

With Love

RECENTLY I WAS CALLED UPON TO OFFICIATE AT THE 90TH birthday of one of my congregants, a tiny, quiet lady who has survived four ministers, all of whom she loved—except one, and that one she has conveniently dropped from the ranks of memory in order not to have reason to think unkindly of him. She has most decidedly watched me grow over the years and has provided for me a full-blown fan club among her friends and family, for when I arrived at her party I was greeted as a prized guest by people who had never laid eyes on me before that day.

As the event progressed I watched with increasing awe the complete love and devotion poured out toward this unassuming little woman. She who had never dreamed of any great place for herself had inspired the lawyers and teachers among her family. She loved them all unstintingly, and they returned that love entirely, from the most silver-haired senior to the grade-schoolers. I had felt that it was her spiritual belief system which had taught her to give so freely, but I came to see that it was simply an agreeable structure to make recognizable something she had always deeply known, a mental framework upon which to hang her hat, so to speak.

I seriously doubt that this small being is very conversant with the term *unconditional love,* but she demonstrates it more completely than anyone I have ever known. Indeed, she does not seem to know how to do anything else. Small wonder that, at their communal sharing, her family wept—with love!

The life that has not loved has not lived, it is still dead. Love is the sole impulse for creation, and the man who does not have love as the greatest incentive in his life has never developed the real creative instinct.

Ernest Holmes
The Science of Mind

Blended Families

THE TERM *BLENDED FAMILIES* IS VERY MUCH A PART OF OUR 21st century nomenclature. Blending families almost sounds like making a cake, getting all the ingredients together to fill their proper roles so the completed mix looks like something different than any of the original ingredients. No...blended families do not work that way. I know. I am part of such a familial scheme. Better, I think, to coin the term *family salads*, because it is closer to the mark.

No one in families these days becomes part of a non-recognizable mix. Each member, whether by birth or inclusion, is most definitely an individual, and if parents are committed and lucky, they can assist all in belonging to a flexible confederation whose bylaws are love.

I discovered a most interesting thing during my tenure as mother/stepmother: My lack of shared DNA with my stepchildren did not preclude my parenting of them. I could be their mother of sorts, without diminishing the role of their natural mother. I simply provided one more support person to be on their team, and, of course, my children gained the same advantage in their lives.

It's not effortless, not by any means. The tendency to "sort out" loyalties is great for a while, and every now and again I would wonder if I had the largeness of soul or the generosity of spirit to give as much to children not born to me as to those who were. The chosen decision to love without setting boundaries of bloodlines becomes entirely rewarding. When it comes down to it, I figure that we need all the people loving us we can get.

Moving beyond myself is actually an inward journey.
Moving within is the journey toward spirituality.

John Bradshaw
Bradshaw On: The Family

On My Birthday

TODAY IS MY BIRTHDAY, AND I'VE BEEN DOING WHAT I TRY to remember to do at each year's hallmark. I've already gotten over the shock that I'm a year closer to the next Big Decade than I was yesterday and that I most probably have a lot more physical past than future. Now I'm considering my multidimensionality and smiling at the awareness that a part of me is as young as the newest newborn while some of me is brilliantly novaing with a far-off exploding star. Such things must be if this is a cohesive universe.

I ask myself: Did I enjoy myself this past year? Did I learn a few things? Did I actually apologize when it was needed and mean it? Did I purposely take on some consciousness-raising practices and see some real results? Did I have enough courage to take some fearsome risks? Did I succeed sometimes, and on the other hand, did I also fail as well? Did I do some wild things that my normally conservative nature would eschew? Perhaps most important of all, did I love enough to be

145

silent now and again and let others figure things out for themselves?

Since the answers to my annual quiz all happen to be "yes" this time, I'd say I'm having a pretty good day. I know I'm feeling very close to the presence of God right now, and so I'll be looking forward to my next annual checkup. And why not? Consider the alternative!

Watching the moon
at dawn,
solitary, mid-sky,
I know myself completely:
no part left out.

Izumi Shikibu
The Enlightened Heart

Who Smiles?

My loved one touches me
And all that was starched and rigid
Softens into tiny, flowing rivers in my soul.
I recognize the gentle hand,
A callus here, a bit of scarring there,
But the touch is broader than I remember.
Is it He who touches me?

My little one smiles her sidelong smile
And bemuses me with innocent eyes
Crinkled to begin a torrent of giggles,
I know this baby's laughter
Rising in tides of little girl liberties.
But do I note a warmer wideness in this child?
Is it She who smiles at me?

I walk more easily now
Than I did as a youngster,
My step lighter.
A glide rather than a plod.

147

I'm buoyed by what I know of life, of self.
But does a longer stride overstep my small footwork?
Does my Self keep pace with me?

References

Beecher, Evelyn
Beecher's Features, vol. 13
Self Published, 1993
Berkeley, CA

Bendall, George
Collected Essays of George Bendall
DeVorss & Co., 1994
Marina Del Rey, CA

Boone, J. Allen
Kinship With All Life
HarperCollins, 1954
San Francisco, CA

Bradshaw, John
Bradshaw On: The Family
Health Communications, Inc., 1988
Deerfield Beach, FL

Bryant, William
Quantum Politics
New Issues Press, 1993
Western Michigan University
Kalamazoo, MI

Buscaglia, Leo
Love
Ballantine Books, 1972
New York, NY

Capra, Fritjof and David Steindl-Rast
Belonging to the Universe
HarperSanFrancisco, 1991
San Francisco, CA

Christensen, Carl
The Green Bible
Johnny Publishing, 1990
Ben Lomond, CA

The Dalai Lama
Oceans of Wisdom
Harper San Francisco, 1990
San Francisco, CA

De Foore, Bill
Anger: Deal with it, Heal with it
Health Communications, 1991
Deerfield Beach, FL

Dickinson, Emily
The Enlightened Heart
Edited by Stephen Mitchell
Harper & Row, 1989
New York, NY

Fox, Matthew
The Coming of the Cosmic Christ
Harper & Row, 1988
San Francisco, CA

Fulghum, Robert
Uh-Oh
Villard Books, 1991
New York, NY

Holmes, Ernest
The Anatomy of Healing Prayer
DeVorss & Co., 1991
Marina Del Rey, CA

Holmes, Ernest
The Science of Mind
Jeremy P. Tarcher, Inc., 1938
New York, NY

Holmes, Fenwicke
Being and Becoming
Sun Publishing Co., 1993
Santa Fe, NM

The Holy Bible
Revised Standard Version
1 Corinthians 3:16, Isaiah 2:4

Hopkins, Emma Curtis
Scientific Christian Mental Practice
DeVorss & Co., 1974
Marina Del Rey, CA

Houston, Jean
The Search for the Beloved
Jeremy P. Tarcher, Inc., 1987
New York, NY

Issa
The Enlightened Heart
Edited by Stephen Mitchell
Harper & Row, 1989
New York, NY

Jampolsky, Gerald
Love is Letting Go of Fear
Celestial Arts, 1979
Berkeley, CA

153

Land, George and Beth Jarman
Breakpoint and Beyond
HarperCollins, 1992
New York, NY

Lao-tzu
The Enlightened Heart
Edited by Stephen Mitchell
Harper & Row, 1989
New York, NY

Letters of the Scattered Brotherhood
Edited by Mary Strong
Harper & Row, 1948
Los Angeles, CA

McInnis, Noel
You Are an Environment
Reprinted by the North American Association for
Environmental Education, 1972
Troy, OH

Mechtild of Magdeburg
The Enlightened Heart
Edited by Stephen Mitchell
Harper & Row, 1989
New York, NY

1000 Inspirational Things
Compiled by Audrey Stone Morris
Spencer Press, 1958
New York, NY

Rilke, Rainer Maria
The Enlightened Heart
Edited by Stephen Mitchell
Harper & Row, 1989
New York, NY

Shikibu, Izumi
The Enlightened Heart
Edited by Stephen Mitchell
Harper & Row, 1989
New York, NY

Standing Bear, Luther
The Spiritual Athlete
Compiled & Edited by Ray Berry
Joshua Press, 1992
Olema, CA

Stortz, Margaret
Flights Into Life
Self Published, 1969
El Cerrito, CA

Thurman, Howard
With Head and Heart
Harcourt Brace Jovanovich, 1979
Orlando, FL

The Upanishads
The Enlightened Heart
Edited by Stephen Mitchell
Harper & Row, 1989
New York, NY

Whitman, Walt
Leaves of Grass
Barnes & Noble Books, 1993
New York, NY

Wojtyla, Karol
Collected Poems
Random House, 1979
New York, NY

Yeaman, Douglas and Noel McInnis
The Power of Commitment
Science of Mind Publishing, 1990
Los Angeles, CA

Ywahoo, Dhyani
The Spiritual Athlete
Compiled & Edited by Ray Berry
Joshua Press, 1992
Olema, CA

How to Order Tapes

For a list of Dr. Stortz's tapes
and how to order, please write to:

First Church of Religious Science
5000 Clarewood Drive
Oakland, CA 94618
Or call: (510) 547-1979
FAX: (510) 547-2991

Science of Mind
It Will Change Your Life

About the author:

Dr. Margaret Stortz is a Religious Science practitioner and minister of the First Church of Religious Science in Oakland, Calif. For more than 25 years, she has written a column entitled "The Principle in Practice" which appears each month in *Science of Mind* magazine. She is also the author of two books and several pamphlets that describe various aspects of spirituality.

For a list of books by Ernest Holmes, call 1-800-382-6121. Visit Science of Mind Online at http://www.scienceofmind.com.

The award-winning Science of Mind *magazine presents insightful and uplifting articles, interviews, and Daily Guides for Richer Living each month. For more information, call 1-800-247-6463.*

Science of **Mind** ®
A philosophy, a faith, a way of life